CLAUDETTE COLVIN LOOKS BACK ON MARCH 2, 1955:

"When I refused to get out of that bus seat, I knew that I was going to be arrested. The bus driver and the policeman thought that it was just about a bus seat. It wasn't just about a seat. I felt that Jim Crow laws were unfair. I felt that discrimination was unfair, and it wasn't just segregation on the buses, it was a whole lot of other things too—the atmosphere and the way life was back then. The turning point of my life, when I and a lot of other students became aware of prejudice and racism, was when one of my classmates was arrested for a crime many people believed he did not commit. His name was Jeremiah Reeves. He was a very popular student who was crazy about music. Jeremiah played in a local band. I was in ninth grade when he was put in jail."

OTHER PUFFIN BOOKS YOU MAY ENJOY

Charlie Pippin   Candy Dawson Boyd

Chevrolet Saturdays   Candy Dawson Boyd

A Different Beat   Candy Dawson Boyd

Forever Friends   Candy Dawson Boyd

Freedom Songs   Yvette Moore

Growin'   Nikki Grimes

The Hundred Penny Box   Sharon Bell Mathis

Just Like Martin   Ossie Davis

Just My Luck   Emily Moore

Let the Circle Be Unbroken   Mildred D. Taylor

Listen for the Fig Tree   Sharon Bell Mathis

Ludie's Song   Dirlie Herlihy

My Black Me   Arnold Adoff, editor

My Life with Martin Luther King, Jr.   Coretta Scott King

The Road to Memphis   Mildred D. Taylor

Roll of Thunder, Hear My Cry   Mildred D. Taylor

Sidewalk Story   Sharon Bell Mathis

Something to Count On   Emily Moore

Take a Walk in Their Shoes   Glennette Tilley Turner

WITNESSES
TO FREEDOM

Young People Who Fought for Civil Rights

Belinda Rochelle

PUFFIN BOOKS

PUFFIN BOOKS
Published by the Penguin Group
Penguin Books USA Inc., 375 Hudson Street, New York, New York 10014, U.S.A.
Penguin Books Ltd, 27 Wrights Lane, London W8 5TZ, England
Penguin Books Australia Ltd, Ringwood, Victoria, Australia
Penguin Books Canada Ltd, 10 Alcorn Avenue, Toronto, Ontario, Canada M4V 3B2
Penguin Books (N.Z.) Ltd, 182–190 Wairau Road, Auckland 10, New Zealand

Penguin Books Ltd, Registered Offices: Harmondsworth, Middlesex, England

First published in the United States of America by Lodestar Books, an affiliate of
Dutton Children's Books, a division of Penguin Books USA Inc., 1993
Published simultaneously in Canada by McClelland & Stewart, Toronto
Published in Puffin Books, 1997

10 9 8 7 6 5 4 3 2 1

THE LIBRARY OF CONGRESS HAS CATALOGED THE LODESTAR EDITION AS FOLLOWS:

Rochelle, Belinda.
Witnesses to freedom: young people who fought for civil rights / Belinda Rochelle.—1st ed.
    p.   cm.
Includes bibliographical references and index.
Summary: Describes the experiences of young blacks who were involved in significant events in the
civil rights movement, including Brown vs. Board of Education, the Montgomery bus boycott, and the
sit-in movement.
ISBN 0-525-67377-6
1. Afro-Americans—Civil rights—Juvenile literature. 2. Civil rights workers—United States—
Biography—Juvenile literature. 3. Afro-Americans—Biography—Juvenile literature. 4. Civil rights
movements—United States—History—20th century—Juvenile literature.[1. Civil rights movements—
History. 2. Afro-Americans—Civil rights. 3. Race relations.] I. Title.
E185.61.R69 1993
323.1'196073—dc20 93-16165 CIP AC

Puffin Books ISBN 0-14-038432-4

Printed in the United States of America

to the strong and proud women in my life:
my mother, Hattie; my daughter, Shevon;
my best friend, Deborah; and my editor,
Rosemary Brosnan, for her enduring faith
and patience

CONTENTS

PREFACE

Most of you have heard about people who were involved in the civil rights movement. Martin Luther King, Jr., Ralph Abernathy, and Rosa Parks are a few of the adults who inspired others in the struggle for equality. But many kinds of people spearheaded the civil rights movement—young and old, black and white, students and ministers—common people coming together for common goals. The civil rights movement was not successful because of one man or one woman—it was successful because of the collective action of many people.

I wrote *Witnesses to Freedom* because I felt there were some people in the civil rights movement whose stories demanded special attention—children, thousands of children, some as young as six, who marched side by side with adults in this struggle for freedom. We will never know all of their names, and most of their pictures will not be in history books, but without young people the civil rights movement could not have succeeded.

In *Witnesses to Freedom*, you'll meet some of these courageous children, learn about their stories, and share their battles as they shape the history of a nation.

ACKNOWLEDGMENTS

Librarians helped extensively with this project. I would like to thank the librarians at Takoma Park Library, Washington, D.C.; Martin Luther King, Jr., Library, Washington, D.C.; Library of Congress, Washington, D.C.; Birmingham Public Library, Birmingham, Alabama.

The quotation from *The Trumpet of Conscience* by Martin Luther King, Jr., on page xi, copyright 1966 by Harper and Row, is reprinted by permission of The Joan Daves Agency.

The quotations on pages 18, 40, and 55, from "The Burning Truth in the South," by Martin Luther King, Jr., appeared in the May 1960 issue of *The Progressive*. Reprinted by permission from *The Progressive*, 409 East Main Street, Madison, Wisconsin 53703.

The "Letter from Birmingham City Jail" from *Why We Can't Wait* by Martin Luther King, Jr., on pages 59–60, copyright 1963 by Harper and Row, is reprinted by permission from The Joan Daves Agency.

The excerpt from the "I Have a Dream" speech, on page 71, copyright 1963 by Martin Luther King, Jr., copyright renewed 1991 by Coretta Scott King, is reprinted by permission of The Joan Daves Agency.

"The blanket of fear was lifted by Negro youth. When they took their struggle to the streets, a new spirit of resistance was born. Inspired by the boldness and ingenuity of Negroes, white youth stirred into action and formed an alliance that aroused the conscience of the nation."

—Martin Luther King, Jr.

O N E

Barbara Johns and R.R. Moton High School

Barbara Johns was cold. It was hard to concentrate on her teacher, Miss Davenport, when the temperature in the school was almost freezing. The winter coat she wore did little to keep her warm.

R.R. Moton High School in Farmville, Virginia, was a very small school. Some students were forced to attend classes in one of three small shacks on the school grounds. The books that the students read were worn; some of the pages were torn or missing. Many times there were not enough books for each student. The school bus was old and unheated, and it often broke down. It was 1951, Barbara's third year at R.R. Moton High School. Not much had changed since she started attending R.R. Moton. Barbara knew why conditions at the school were poor: R.R. Moton was the school for black students.

In many places in the United States during the 1950s, black and white people were forced to stay separated. This separation was called segregation. Many states passed laws that legalized segregation in schools and housing. These laws and customs were called Jim Crow, and they prevented blacks and whites from mixing at public facilities such as swimming pools, libraries, and restaurants. Because of the color of their skin, black Americans were not treated fairly or as equal citizens. A black person could use public facilities only at certain times, and never when a white person was using the facilities. Some places were designated by signs that said FOR WHITES ONLY and COLORED ONLY.

In Farmville, Virginia, black students were forced to attend different schools from those that white students attended. The high school that white students attended was clean and warm. All the students had books, and their desks were new. R.R. Moton High School didn't even have a gym or a cafeteria. Barbara Johns felt something had to be done. She went with her parents to town meetings to talk about conditions at the school. They were told that R.R. Moton did not need repairs or school supplies. At meeting after meeting, city officials ignored requests to improve conditions at R.R. Moton. These city officials didn't seem to care about the school or the students. Barbara was disappointed. Her family, especially her uncle, Vernon Johns, had always stressed equality and education. She was taught that the color of one's skin, black or white, did not matter—every U.S. citizen had the right to be treated fairly.

All U.S. citizens have certain rights of personal freedom guaranteed by the Constitution. These rights are called civil rights. Every citizen has the right to a decent, fair education; the right to vote; and the right to use public services and fa-

2

Barbara Johns in her high school graduation photograph.
(Barbara Johns)

cilities. The civil rights of black students were being ignored by city officials. How could the black students receive a good education when they were treated unfairly? Barbara decided she had to do something and she knew who would help her—the other students who attended R.R. Moton.

3

Barbara Johns

I enjoyed school, but I didn't like the conditions at the school. The entire student body totaled 450 students, and when we decided to boycott classes, we used a small tar-paper shack as our headquarters. I was just sixteen years old, but I felt like we had to do something.

People ask me who my heroes were. I have to answer that I had no nationally known or recognized idols, but my instructors were my heroes. I especially liked Miss Davenport. Our instructors would have to do things like start the wood stoves before they taught classes—things janitors would be responsible for in the white schools.

The students came up with ten demands. Most were improvements to the school. We wanted simple things, like new books and new desks. I wasn't the only student upset

The students decided to organize a boycott of the school. Students would walk out of school and not return until conditions were improved. Barbara knew that the principal and teachers would disapprove of a boycott, so she figured out a way to get the principal to leave the school: A student called the principal and reported that two truant students needed to be picked up at the train station. After the principal left the school, Barbara contacted each teacher and pre-

about school conditions. Almost every student at Moton participated in the boycott. That's why everybody—our parents, our teachers, everyone—became motivated to find solutions to our school condition.

Since what happened at the school directly affected the students, I felt that what students did in terms of protest should directly affect the school. I was not afraid. I was not in Virginia when the Ku Klux Klan allegedly burned the cross in front of my home. By that time I was in Montgomery, Alabama. But every black person in the South was aware of the presence of danger.

My advice to young people today is that children should recognize their own self-worth. Always seek the best way to do things and, most of all, strive toward excellence.

Barbara Johns, a former teacher, lived in Philadelphia, Pennsylvania, until her death in September 1991.

tended that the principal wanted all students to meet in the auditorium for a school assembly.

When everyone gathered in the auditorium, Barbara walked up onto the stage. The teachers became suspicious. Where was the principal? Why was Barbara Johns on stage alone? One of the teachers tried to force Barbara off the stage, but other students stopped the teacher. All the students liked Barbara, and they wanted to hear her speak.

R.R. Moton students at an assembly in the school auditorium. *(Library of Congress: USN & WR Collection)*

She talked about the poor conditions at R.R. Moton High School and told the students that they must do something about them. She announced the plan to boycott. Many of the students agreed. On April 23, 1951, the students marched out of the school, led by Barbara.

"But it was the right thing to do," Barbara explained to her worried parents as they sat huddled in the living room. "What can they do?"

Her father, Robert, shook his head. He was concerned about Barbara. She didn't understand the danger she was in. "You're going to have to leave Farmville; it's too dangerous for you to be here," he said.

Most of the students' parents did not think the boycott was a good idea. Many white people disapproved of the boycott and threatened to put the students in jail. Members of the Klu Klux Klan (KKK), an organization of white men and women who hate other people because of differences in skin color, race, and religion, were angry. Many city officials and police officers belonged to the Ku Klux Klan. They did not like Barbara and the other R.R. Moton students who were trying to change the school system.

"You're going to have to live with your Uncle Vernon in Montgomery, until things are back to normal," Barbara's father said.

That night Barbara left Farmville and went to live with her uncle in Alabama. A few nights after the boycott began, members of the Ku Klux Klan placed a burning cross in front of the Johns's home as a warning. This act of hatred

Barbara Johns became a teacher and worked in Philadelphia public schools for many years. *(Barbara Johns)*

did not stop the young students of R.R. Moton. The boycott continued for two weeks.

In May 1951, a month after the boycott started, the R.R. Moton students, with the help of lawyers from the National Association for the Advancement of Colored People

(NAACP), filed a lawsuit. This lawsuit demanded not only the improvement of the school's conditions but also the desegregation of all of Farmville's schools, so that white and black students could attend the same schools.

Five years later, city officials closed all schools in Farmville to prevent them from being integrated. All the students living in Farmville had to attend schools outside of Prince Edward County, Virginia. Soon protests would begin all around the country. Organizations like the National Association for the Advancement of Colored People worked to end discrimination and segregation in all places, including schools. Many people would begin to protest against segregation in peaceful, nonviolent ways, by marching and boycotting places that treated black people unfairly. Some laws and customs would have to change, because not everyone in the United States believed in equality. The struggle had just begun, but many people, including young students like Barbara Johns, would fight the battle for civil rights.

T W O

Brown v. Board of Education

"We conclude that in the field of public education the
doctrine of 'separate but equal' has no place. Separate
educational facilities are inherently unequal."

—United States Supreme Court
Brown v. *Board of Education* decision

Eleven-year-old Spottswood Thomas Bolling, Jr., sat
close to his older brother, Wannamaker, as his parents faced the principal of Sousa Junior High School.
Spottswood didn't want to admit to Wannamaker that he
was afraid, but when Wannamaker squirmed in his chair so
did Spottswood.

When he was sure no one was watching, Spottswood
glanced down the hallway of Sousa Junior High School. It
was a beautiful school, close to his home. Spottswood,
Wannamaker, and three other black students wanted to attend Sousa but were not admitted to the school because it
was for whites only. The five students were forced to attend overcrowded Shaw Junior High, the school for black
students.

* * *

"One block . . . two blocks . . . three blocks . . ." Linda Brown counted out loud as she passed each street. She held her father's hand tightly as they started their long walk to her school.

"Five blocks . . ." she counted as she passed Sumner Elementary School. She hesitated in front of the school.

Schools were also segregated in Topeka, Kansas, where Linda attended Monroe School. Monroe School was twenty blocks from her home. Every day Linda walked over a dangerous railroad crossing to attend the school for black students, even though Sumner Elementary School was closer. Oliver Brown, Linda's father, filed a lawsuit, *Brown* v. *Board of Education of Topeka, Kansas,* to force school officials to allow Linda to attend Sumner.

While those who were waging the fight for civil rights took to the streets in peaceful, nonviolent protest, the battle was also being fought in the nation's courts. Most segregation laws affected the country's public school system. Only sixteen states prohibited segregated schools.

The Supreme Court is the highest court in the United States. The Court decides if laws comply with the Constitution. Segregation of schools and other public facilities was legal, according to the Supreme Court case of *Plessy* v. *Ferguson.* This court decision, which was passed down in 1896, said that separate facilities for blacks and whites were legal as long as the facilities were equal. Many experts felt that *Plessy* v. *Ferguson* had to be overturned before desegre- **11**

Spottswood Thomas Bolling, Jr.

Of course we knew, even as children, the importance of the court cases. Every case that was filed in court was reviewed by lawyers from the NAACP to see if there was a chance that the case would be successful.

There was a lot of pressure on the families and especially on the students. I was expected to be perfect, and there's no such thing as a perfect child. I had to be on my best behavior. I wore nice clothes, and when we were out in public places I could not get dirty. I remember that someone came up to me at Spingarn after the principal made the

gation could be accomplished. Most of the schools for black students were deteriorating, teachers did not receive decent salaries, and books and equipment were often old and outdated. Schoolchildren were not only separated by race, but the quality of schools for black students was not comparable to the quality of white students' schools.

Most of the participants in the civil rights movement felt that schools could be equal only if all schools were integrated and black and white students attended the same schools. Many black parents were upset by the poor quality of their children's education. Some families in different areas of the United States even filed lawsuits to change the "separate but equal" laws.

announcement, but I was very shy. Newspaper people came to the school to ask me how I felt. I just nodded my head and went out to the playground and played baseball. I was so quiet and shy that I stayed out on the playground until dark, hoping the newspaper people would just go away. I tried to pretend that it all didn't mean anything, but to a lot of people it meant everything. My mother told me that I was a part of history. But to me, every student forced to attend segregated schools was a part of history.

Spottswood Thomas Bolling, Jr., worked for the District of Columbia government. He remained active in community affairs up until his death in 1990.

Many of these civil rights cases were argued in local courts as well as in state courts; gradually, many of the cases came before the United States Supreme Court for review. The justices of the Supreme Court decided to combine six of the many cases that challenged the "separate but equal" policies of the nation's educational system. They chose *Brown* v. *Board of Education of Topeka, Kansas* as the first case. *Davis* v. *County School Board of Prince Edward County*— the case from Farmville, Virginia, and the students of R.R. Moton—was added, along with four other cases, including Spottswood's case, *Bolling* v. *Sharpe*. The justices combined the cases under the name of the first case, *Brown* v. *Board of Education of Topeka, Kansas.*

Making history: Spottswood Bolling, Jr., and his mother, Sarah, celebrating the *Brown v. Board of Education* decision. (*Martin Luther King, Jr., Library*/Washington Star *collection*)

This court case was one that attorney Thurgood Marshall and fellow attorneys of the NAACP Legal Defense Fund had prepared for more than ten years. The lawyers had won **14** several cases that allowed black students to integrate universities, but they had not yet won a case to desegregate public elementary and high schools. Most people felt that if the United States Supreme Court ordered the end of segregation in schools, then segregation might end in other places as well.

The Supreme Court delivered its ruling on May 17, 1954. The majority decision declared that segregated schools were unequal, and that this policy was unconstitutional. The decision guaranteed the rights of black and white students to a fair and equal education.

Dr. Williams, the principal of Spingarn High School in Washington, D.C., made an announcement about the Supreme Court ruling to his students. Spottswood sat quietly in his chair. Four years after his parents had filed the lawsuit, the decision had finally been made. Many things had changed during those years. His brother, Wannamaker, was out of school. Spottswood was now a freshman at Spingarn. For a few minutes all of the students sat quietly as if they could not believe the news. Then everyone started to talk at once.

On Tuesday, September 14, 1954, 165 schools in the Washington, D.C., area were integrated without trouble. Spottswood joined more than three thousand students who were transferred out of overcrowded schools and placed in seventeen previously segregated schools.

Many states refused to obey the Court's order to desegregate. In Mississippi, whites formed hate groups such as the **15**

Signs of change: Many schools and students accepted the Supreme Court decision to integrate schools without violence. *(Library of Congress: USN & WR Collection)*

Citizens Council to keep black students from integrating schools. Like the Ku Klux Klan, the Citizens Council sometimes used violence to frighten black and white people who supported desegregation. Because many schools refused to integrate, the Supreme Court issued another ruling on May 31, 1955, ordering public schools to desegregate "with all deliberate speed." Schools in Farmville, Virginia—Barbara Johns's hometown—were closed. In some places, white parents removed their children from public schools and enrolled them in private schools that did not allow integration.

Resistance to integrating public schools occurred not only in southern states but also in northern states, where many schools were also segregated. More than ten years would pass before most schools in the United States obeyed the Supreme Court's decision.

T H R E E

The Little Rock Nine

"It was the high school, college and elementary
school young people who were in the front line of
the school desegregation struggle. Lest it be forgotten,
the opening of hundreds of schools to Negroes for the first
time in history required that there be young Negroes
with the moral and physical courage to face the
challenges and, all too frequently, the mortal danger
presented by mob resistance."

—Martin Luther King, Jr.

Elizabeth Eckford glanced at her reflection in the mirror. The dress that her mother had made for this special day was beautiful. It was her first day at a new high school and she was nervous. She looked at the clock. It was almost time to meet her friends.

Elizabeth nervously set off for school. When she stepped off the bus, she faced a large, angry crowd of white people and hundreds of soldiers.

Because the United States Supreme Court had prohibited segregation, many schools were forced to admit black students. Some schools obeyed the federal order and desegregated immediately, allowing black students to attend

Elizabeth Eckford faced a jeering crowd as she tried to enter Central High School in Little Rock, Arkansas. *(UPI/Bettmann Newsphotos)*

Elizabeth Eckford

What many people don't realize is that there were many black children like us who had to integrate schools. We weren't unusual, even though our situation received a lot of attention. We were not the only black students who were harassed—it was happening in other schools all over the country. The year we attended [Central] was a difficult year. Most of the white students didn't bother us; they just pretended that we didn't even exist. But there was this small group of white students that bothered us every day. They would call us names, trip us in the hallways, and push us down the steps, without fear of being reprimanded by the teachers or the principal. We couldn't fight back; we couldn't even say anything to provoke confrontation because it might result in our being expelled. And that might mean the end of any integration efforts at Central High School.

Every day it was something, and often I cried because of the torment that my parents and I went through. I remem-

previously all-white schools. But in most cities, officials refused to comply with the federal order. Arkansas and Texas were the only two states in the South that tried to obey the Supreme Court decision.

School officials in Little Rock, Arkansas, planned to desegregate the local high school in 1957 by admitting a small

ber one incident in particular. Carlotta [Walls] and I were waiting for our parents in the school corridor. I remember my father walking up to the school to escort me to the car. The crowd began to pelt him with rocks. I felt so frightened and helpless watching him. He was so brave. It helped me to understand that even though there was a screaming mob outside of that school every day, there were a lot more people—families and people that I didn't know—who supported us.

I found comfort from the other black students. We were very close friends because we had to depend on one another. Thanks to a number of people, especially our parents, we never forgot the reasons we were attending Central High School. It was up to us to make integration a success, and if you think about it that way, then you realize that when you believe in something, even if you're afraid, you'll find a way to accomplish your goals.

Elizabeth Eckford still resides in Little Rock, Arkansas.

number of black students to Central, the school for white students. Originally, seventy-five black students registered to attend. After a review by the Little Rock school board, only nine students were allowed to enroll, including Elizabeth Eckford, Jefferson Thomas, Gloria Ray, Thelma Mothershed, Melba Patillo, Terrance Roberts, Carlotta Walls,

Ernest Green, and Minniejean Brown. These nine students became known as the "Little Rock Nine." Daisy Bates, the president of the Arkansas NAACP and the editor of a local newspaper, served as an advisor to the black students.

Local officials tried to plan a smooth transition, but the governor of Arkansas, Orval Faubus, refused to cooperate. He did not approve of integration and promised to place the National Guard, a state military force, at the school to keep out all black students.

Many people supported the governor. On the first day of school, hundreds of people gathered outside of the school to prevent the Little Rock Nine from entering Central.

Elizabeth faced the angry crowd alone. She did not see the other black students because Daisy Bates had decided to take them to school on their first day. She had told the students and their families to meet at her house before going to Central High School, but she had been unable to get in touch with Elizabeth because the Eckfords didn't have a telephone.

When Elizabeth tried to walk to the main entrance of the school, the angry crowd followed her. Some people spat at her. She walked toward the National Guardsmen, thinking the soldiers would help her get into the school, but the guardsmen blocked her from entering.

"Nigger!" a woman screamed at her.

"We don't want niggers in our school!" another hollered at Elizabeth.

22   Elizabeth tried to ignore the mob, but the angry crowd

KEEP OUR WHITE SCHOOLS WHITE!

TONIGHT AND EVERY NIGHT 'TILL SCHOOL OPENS
(Except Sunday)

IMPORTANT MEETING

TO KEEP THE NIGGERS OUT OF WHITE SCHOOLS

AT THE COURT HOUSE
ON THE SQUARE - 7:00 P.M.

FIND OUT WHAT BEN WEST, FRANK CLEMENT AND
BENNY'S NASHVILLE SCHOOL BOARD ARE DOING TO
RUIN NASHVILLE FOREVER.

SAVE YOUR KIDS! PREVENT RACE RIOTS,
MURDER, DYNAMITINGS, AND HANGINGS!

BRING YOUR FRIENDS EVERY EVENING

AT 7:00 P.M. TO COURTHOURSE ON THE SQUARE.

HONOR-PRIDE-FIGHT-SAVE THE WHITES

**The Citizens Council and the Ku Klux Klan distributed posters like this one
to recruit members.** *(Library of Congress: USN & WR Collection)*

As Jefferson Thomas, one of the Little Rock Nine, waited for a bus, a crowd taunted and threatened him. *(UPI/Bettmann Newsphotos)*

followed her as she ran to a bench. She felt an arm around her. It was a newspaper reporter; he told Elizabeth not to cry. Then a white woman, Grace Lorch, helped Elizabeth board a bus home. Later that morning, the eight other black students tried to enter Central High, but they could not get past the screaming mob and the National Guardsmen.

Two weeks later, the students met at Daisy Bates's home to plan another attempt to enter Central. This time the Little Rock Nine got into the school, but a mob of over a thousand angry people gathered outside. Some members of the mob invaded the school. Fearing for the safety of the children, the principal sent all students home.

Finally, the president of the United States, Dwight Eisenhower, ordered federal troops to Arkansas to guard the Little Rock Nine. Each student was assigned a soldier for protection. But even with the soldiers there as bodyguards, the black students were often tripped or called names as they walked through the hallways.

When Minniejean Brown was selected to sing in the glee club, a group of white parents forced school officials to keep Minniejean out of the club.

There were other incidents as well. Someone threw a bomb at Carlotta Walls's home. Sometimes the students received threatening telephone calls in the middle of the night. Every time Ernest Green raised his hand to answer a teacher's question, he was ignored. Some of the white students were friendly to the black students and invited their black classmates to eat lunch with them. But every day the

Federal troops escorted the Little Rock Nine to all of their classes at Central High School. *(UPI/Bettman News photos)*

Little Rock Nine had to face the angry mobs waiting for them outside the school. At the end of the school year, Ernest Green became the first black student to graduate from Central High School.

The following year Governor Faubus closed Central High School to prevent any further attempts to integrate the school. Today, many years after the *Brown* v. *Board of Education* case, most schools in the United States do, in fact, remain segregated.

F O U R

The Montgomery Bus Boycott

"Make a career of humanity. Commit yourself to the
noble struggle for equal rights. You will make a greater
person of yourself, a greater nation of your country,
and a finer world to live in."

—Martin Luther King, Jr.
Congressional Record 105
(20 May 1959): 8696–97

Fifteen-year-old Claudette Colvin shifted the English, math, and science books in her arms. She had lots of homework and had to carry all of her textbooks to study for Friday morning exams.

Claudette stepped off the sidewalk and peered down the street to see if the bus was coming. She was anxious to get home, but the bus was nowhere in sight. Fifteen minutes passed and just as Claudette thought she couldn't wait another minute longer the Montgomery Transit bus moved up the street toward her. It was March 2, 1955, a day that would change Claudette's life forever.

Claudette paid her fare and boarded the city bus. Since it was five o'clock, many people were heading home from work. As more passengers boarded, the bus quickly filled and soon no more seats were left. At one stop, a white man got on the bus. Because the bus was crowded, the man was forced to stand.

The bus driver stopped the bus and walked to where Claudette was sitting.

"Get up. Give up your seat, girl." Claudette looked at the bus driver, and then glanced around her.

The bus driver raised an eyebrow. "Get up," he repeated. "You coloreds give up those seats right now."

The pregnant woman sitting next to Claudette stood.

"I'm sorry but I am not going to give up my seat," Claudette informed the bus driver.

"This white man here needs a seat and he's gonna have one—the one you're sitting in." The bus driver got off the bus and waved down a police car.

Three policemen boarded the bus and pulled Claudette out of her seat. She began to scream as they handcuffed her and dragged her off the bus into the back of the police car to take her to jail. She could feel the tears in her throat, and she gasped for air. She was so angry she could barely breathe.

The police car slowed down as it passed some of Claudette's classmates. The students were talking and laughing, and then they saw her, sitting in the backseat of the police car. Soon everyone would know that she had been arrested. She couldn't hold back her tears any longer. She not only felt angry, she felt ashamed.

In Montgomery, Alabama, the law stated that although **29**

black passengers paid the same fares as white passengers, black passengers had to sit in the rear of the bus and give up their seats if a white passenger had nowhere else to sit. On city buses black people could not even sit next to white people. After black passengers paid their fare, they then had to get off the bus and reenter through the back door. Sometimes bus drivers would drive away before the passengers reboarded the bus. Sometimes drivers cursed at and spat on them. Even when there were empty seats in the front of the bus they were forced to stand.

Jo Ann Robinson and members of the Women's Political Council (WPC), an organization of black women, met many times with city officials to talk about the treatment of black passengers on public buses. The city officials refused to make any changes. Instead, passengers like Claudette continued to be dragged off the buses and put in jail.

Claudette's family called Rosa Parks and E.D. Nixon. Rosa Parks was Claudette's friend and an NAACP youth advisor, and E.D. Nixon was the president of the local chapter of the NAACP. Rosa Parks raised the money to get Claudette out of jail, and E.D. Nixon got the young girl a lawyer. Claudette was found guilty of breaking the law and was ordered to pay a fine.

After being released from jail, Claudette was determined to remain involved in the fight for civil rights. She joined the Youth Council of the NAACP, but Claudette heard people whispering about her. To some students and the older people in the black community, Claudette was a troublemaker. Their disapproval bothered her, and she soon had difficulty concentrating on her schoolwork. Claudette was upset. Little had changed since her arrest. She did not feel like she belonged. She wouldn't talk to any of her classmates. She changed her hair to a natural style, refusing to wear it the way her friends did. Rejected by her classmates, neighbors, and some members of her family, Claudette dropped out of school. She moved to New York City, where she lived with relatives.

Nine months after Claudette's arrest, someone else remembered the many brave people like Claudette who had been mistreated on the Montgomery buses. On December 1, 1955, Rosa Parks boarded a bus to go home. When a white passenger got on the bus, the bus driver ordered Rosa Parks to give up her seat. It was not the first time the same bus driver had forced Mrs. Parks to stand up. But this time Mrs. Parks refused to move. The bus driver called the police, and two officers arrested Mrs. Parks. Like Claudette Colvin, Rosa Parks was thrown in jail.

The black people of Montgomery decided that something must be done to change the unfair bus segregation laws. Rosa Parks and other leaders in the community chose to protest the law. Mrs. Parks filed a lawsuit to change the bus segregation laws in Montgomery, Alabama.

Some members of the community formed the Montgomery Improvement Association (MIA), an organization dedicated to changing the public transportation laws and regulations. The Montgomery Improvement Association de- **31**

Claudette Colvin

When I refused to get out of that bus seat, I knew that I was going to be arrested. The bus driver and the policemen thought that it was just about a bus seat. It wasn't just about a seat. I felt that Jim Crow laws were unfair. I felt that discrimination was unfair, and it wasn't just segregation on the buses, it was a whole lot of other things too—the atmosphere and the way life was back then. The turning point of my life, when I and a lot of other students became aware of prejudice and racism, was when one of my classmates was arrested for a crime many people believed he did not commit. His name was Jeremiah Reeves. He was a very popular student who was crazy about music. Jeremiah played in a local band. I was in the ninth grade when he was put in jail.

Blacks were often put in jail for crimes they did not commit. Black Americans were forced to live under these

cided that black people should not ride the buses if they were not treated fairly. In Montgomery, most of the people who rode the buses were black, so if they refused to ride the bus company would lose lots of money.

For the boycott to work, every black person would have to stay off the buses. Black elementary and high school students passed out fliers about the boycott to every black person in Montgomery. With the students' help, thousands of

32

conditions. Segregation meant you couldn't go where you wanted to go. All black people were treated like they were not human beings. Most students wanted to know the reasons why segregation and discrimination were a part of our lives. So naturally, because we were students, many of us talked about this in school. Some teachers did not want to talk about it, but others talked about black history. I really believed that civil rights wasn't about our skin color; it was as simple as what is right and what is wrong, what is fair and what is unfair.

I wasn't the popular girl in school. I didn't live with my family—I lived with my grandmother. I was very skinny and tall, and I wore thick glasses. I felt like an outsider, but it didn't matter. Even if I had to do it, stay in that seat and go to jail, then I had to do it. But it wasn't for me, it wasn't just for me—it was for people like Jeremiah Reeves.

Claudette Colvin lives in New York City. She works as a nurse's aide.

fliers reached all of the black neighborhoods in Montgomery. The flier said:

> . . . Don't ride the buses to work, to town, to school, or anywhere on Monday. You can afford to stay out of school for one day if you have no other way to go except by bus. You can also afford to stay out of town for one day. If you work, take a cab, or walk. But please, children and grown-ups, don't ride the bus at all on Monday.

Martin Luther King, Jr., the young minister of a local church, was voted the leader of the Montgomery bus boycott by the MIA. The son of a Baptist minister, Dr. King was born in Atlanta, Georgia. As a young boy, he learned about segregation. He knew that he could not sit in the front of a city bus or drink from "white" water fountains. Martin even lost a childhood friend when his friend's parents discovered that Martin was black. They did not want their son to play with a black boy.

Martin entered Morehouse College when he was just fifteen years old. After graduation, he went to Crozer Theological Seminary, where he became interested in the teachings of Mahatma Gandhi.

Gandhi was a leader in India. When India was ruled by Britain, Gandhi helped his country gain independence from British rule by using nonviolent protest. When Indians marched or boycotted stores they were beaten and put in jail, but they did not fight back. After many years of struggle, India finally won its independence in 1947.

At Crozer Theological Seminary, King learned everything he could about Gandhi. Now, as the leader of the Montgomery bus boycott, King would use many of Gandhi's tactics of nonviolent protest to create social change.

Dr. King's church, Dexter Avenue Baptist Church, was the headquarters for the boycott organizers. King received many threatening phone calls and letters. The Citizens Council burned crosses on his lawn. He didn't worry about his safety, but he was very worried about his wife, Coretta, and their young daughter, Yolanda.

34

Martin Luther King, Jr., addressing members of the Montgomery Improvement Association.
(Library of Congress)

Rosa Parks Remembers Claudette Colvin

It was especially difficult when our young children were mistreated on the Montgomery buses. You didn't really have to do anything for the bus driver to spit on you or leave you after you were forced to reenter through the back door. Some of the bus drivers were that mean-spirited. Most people didn't have cars, so many of us depended on public transportation. Students sometimes rode the buses to school; adults used the buses to get to and from work and to shop for food and clothing.

I don't know what made Claudette refuse to give up her seat. I guess she was tired—we were all tired of being mistreated for no other reason than because we were black.

Reverend Ralph Abernathy, Dr. King's closest friend and advisor, and Jo Ann Robinson developed a three-point plan to present to city officials. The first demand was that bus drivers treat black passengers with respect. The second demand was that seating should be first come, first served. The third demand was that the company should hire black bus drivers because most of the bus passengers were black. The city officials and the bus company did not accept these demands.

We paid the same fare, and they needed our money to stay in business, but that did not mean that they respected us. That was reflected in their treatment of black passengers.

Claudette was a very nice young lady. She was very quiet and was always well dressed and well mannered. She did very well in school and was a member of the NAACP Youth Council. She changed after she was arrested, though. Being dragged off a bus was a very traumatic experience for anyone, especially a child. When she was found guilty and everybody knew she had a police record, she was treated differently by her classmates. She became withdrawn. She wasn't the same child that we all knew. The effects of discrimination stay with you your entire lifetime.

Rosa Parks lives in Detroit, Michigan, where she remains active in politics.

After the first day of the boycott, thousands of people, including hundreds of students, met at Dexter to decide whether to continue the boycott or not. Martin Luther King, Jr., reported that Rosa Parks had been found guilty of breaking the law. He talked about what had happened to Claudette and other black people who rode the Montgomery buses. The people decided to stay off the buses until the laws were changed.

Members of the Montgomery Improvement Association   **37**

Rosa Parks rode a Montgomery, Alabama, city bus when the boycott ended. *(UPI/Bettmann Newsphotos)*

organized ways to get thousands of black people to and from jobs and schools. Many people walked to work, and others formed car pools, sharing their cars to help others get to work, home, or school.

Some people opposed any changes in the laws that permitted segregation on public transportation. The Ku Klux Klan and the Citizens Council tried to frighten anyone who participated in the boycott. Someone threw a bomb onto Dr.

38

King's front porch. Ralph Abernathy's home and church were also bombed. The Ku Klux Klan marched through Montgomery.

But the boycott continued, lasting thirteen months before the segregation laws were changed. Members of the Montgomery Improvement Association won the right to receive first-come, first-served seating; black men would be hired as drivers for the bus company; and black passengers would be treated fairly and with respect. The success of the Montgomery bus boycott led to boycotts in other Alabama cities, including Mobile, Tuskegee, and Birmingham. After the Montgomery bus boycott, Martin Luther King, Jr., became the director of the Southern Christian Leadership Conference (SCLC), a new civil rights organization. People from all over the world read about the boycott in Montgomery. Rosa Parks, Claudette Colvin, Martin Luther King, Jr., and forty-five thousand brave people who participated in the boycott won one of the first major victories in the civil rights movement.

F I V E

The Sit-in Movement

"Never before in the United States has so large a body of
students spread a struggle over so great an area in pursuit of
a goal of human dignity and freedom."

—Martin Luther King, Jr.

Seventeen-year-old Joseph McNeil sat at the lunch counter at the bus station in Greensboro, North Carolina. The waitress looked at him and frowned.

"We don't serve Negroes at the lunch counter," she snapped and walked away. Lunch counters at most restaurants and bus stations in southern states were segregated.

That night in his dorm room, Joseph told his best friends, Ezell Blair, Jr., Franklin McCain, and David Richmond, about what had happened to him at the lunch counter. The four boys were students at A & T College in Greensboro North Carolina. They were all seventeen, except Franklin, who was eighteen. They were members of the NAACP and spent a lot of their time studying and talking about race relations in the United States. It was not the first time one of the boys had been denied service at the lunch counter. For almost a month the boys had planned a demonstration to protest discrimination at lunch counters.

40

The boys decided that the time had come to begin their plan to challenge the law. Instead of carrying signs or marching, they would just sit down at the counter.

Rather than boycotting or marching, some civil rights activists chose to participate in sit-ins. Sit-ins were a form of peaceful protest that occurred when a person or a group of people entered a segregated facility such as a restaurant and demanded service. The first sit-ins happened in 1948, but the protests were unsuccessful. In 1960, many civil rights organizations began to train young people in nonviolent demonstrations such as sit-ins. The first training sessions were held in Nashville, Tennessee, where hundreds of black college students attended four black colleges. Jim Lawson, a graduate student, trained the first group of students to carry out sit-ins at lunch counters and libraries in Nashville. But before the sit-ins occurred in Nashville, the boys from Greensboro began their own demonstration on February 1, 1960.

That day they met with Ralph Johns, a local white businessman who was a close friend. Ralph told the boys he would help get them out of jail if they were arrested. Joseph, Ezell, Franklin, and David walked into the local Woolworth department store, sat down at the lunch counter, and waited to be served.

The waitress frowned and continued wiping the counter, ignoring the four boys. Like many stores and restaurants in Greensboro, North Carolina, Woolworth did not serve black people at the lunch counter. The boys sat for more than four

41

Lunch counter sit-ins were held in cities across the country. *(UPI/Bettmann Newsphotos)*

hours waiting to be served and did not leave until the restaurant closed for the day. That night, the boys distributed fliers to black high schools and colleges, encouraging other students to join them in their sit-in.

They returned the next day and again sat at the lunch counter. This time more than seventy of their classmates from North Carolina A & T and other students from Bennett College and Dudley High School joined them. After just a

42

few days, the city officials of Greensboro desegregated lunch counters and other public facilities.

College and high school students from across the South read about the Greensboro sit-ins. The sit-in movement spread to cities across the South. Before the students could participate in a sit-in they were trained in how to react to being harassed or attacked while sitting at the counter. They learned what to do if they were hit or if someone tried to force them off their stools and away from the counter. Many students planned their own sit-ins. Some were beaten or jailed. Sometimes white students joined black students in the sit-ins. The students did not fight back even when they were attacked. They just sat quietly at the counters waiting to be served.

Seventeen-year-old Harvey Gantt stared at the newspaper. The news of the sit-in movement in Greensboro was the talk of Charleston, South Carolina, and it was the main topic at the Charleston NAACP Youth Council meeting.

"We've got some of the same problems right here in Charleston, and we could do the same thing," the NAACP Youth Council president said.

"Most of us are seniors in high school. We're the same age as those guys—we can do it too," Harvey replied.

Just a few weeks after the sit-in in Greensboro, North Carolina, members of the Charleston, South Carolina, NAACP Youth Council began their sit-in. Most of the members of the Charleston NAACP Youth Council were high school **43**

Harvey Gantt

We trained for our sit-in in a secret meeting place. We didn't tell our parents, and we couldn't tell our teachers and mentors because we knew what their reactions would be. What parents would want their children exposed to the threat of harm and violence? So we tried to protect our families from our actions because we were very determined, and nobody could stop us. We held practice sessions so we would be prepared for whatever could happen. Of course, some of us were afraid. I thought a lot about what it would be like in jail. I had these pictures in my mind about how dreadful jail was—dark, damp, isolated from everyone. Yet we all felt the cause was so great that most of

juniors and seniors and felt that college students were not the only ones who could participate in the civil rights movement. From a feeling of envy came a new feeling, one of determination. Twenty-four members of the NAACP Youth Council decided to integrate a lunch counter in downtown Charleston as their local civil rights project.

Harvey was nervous. He was afraid that his parents would find out about the sit-in. Harvey was planning to attend college, but if he went to jail, he knew that he might not be able to go to school. The day before the Charleston

44

us overcame any fear. When we were arrested, the police did not put us in a holding cell in the jail. Instead, we were held in a courtroom. Needless to say, our parents were beside themselves with anger and fear. Most of the students were seniors in high school, and our parents were worried about our school records and how the sit-in would affect our chances of going to college. The students actually found their parents' reactions quite amusing. Most of us came from families where we were taught about the civil rights movement, and we couldn't help but feel that in spite of our parents' anger and fear we had also earned their begrudging admiration.

Harvey Gantt is a former mayor of Charlotte, North Carolina. In 1990, he ran an unsuccessful campaign to be the first black senator from North Carolina.

sit-in, the students met for a practice session. They learned to ignore taunts. They also learned how to protect themselves if someone tried to pull them away from the counter. Harvey knew that he was taking a big chance by participating in the sit-in, but when he marched up to the S.H. Kress lunch counter he felt proud. Almost immediately the police came and dragged the students off to the Charleston city jail.

Later that evening, his parents waited for him after he and the other students were released from jail. His father

As a senior in high school, Harvey Gantt organized a sit-in demonstration in his hometown, Charleston, South Carolina. *(UPI/Bettmann Newsphotos)*

began to scold Harvey for his actions, but Harvey knew that his father was also very proud of him. After the Charleston sit-in, Harvey continued to participate in the civil rights movement. He became the first black American to enroll in Clemson, a segregated university in South Carolina.

46   *   *   *

In the spring of 1960, black and white students from all over the country met in Raleigh, North Carolina. They formed the Student Nonviolent Coordinating Committee (SNCC), an organization of high school and college students. With the help of Ella Baker, a director of the Southern Christian Leadership Conference (SCLC), the students planned future civil rights activities. They wanted to figure out how they could contribute to the struggle for freedom.

Some members of the Student Nonviolent Coordinating Committee formed a group called the Freedom Singers. The Freedom Singers were college students who sang across the country to raise money for the civil rights movement and to inform people who lived far away about civil rights activities. "We Shall Overcome" became the theme song of the civil rights movement.

At demonstrations a songleader or a choir would begin a song, then others would join in. In Selma, Alabama, the site of demonstrations for voting rights, the Selma Youth Freedom Choir opened all rallies and mass meetings. Singing was a powerful tool in the effort to dismantle Jim Crow laws and customs.

The agenda of the Student Nonviolent Coordinating Committee included sit-ins across the South to force the desegregation of all public facilities, including public swimming pools and waiting areas at bus stations and train stations. By the end of 1960, more than one hundred sit-ins had taken place in many different cities across the United States.

S I X

The Freedom Rides

The next target of the civil rights movement was segregated interstate public transportation. Interstate transportation involves traveling from a location in one state to a location in another state. Many of the same problems that blacks faced in Montgomery, Alabama, in 1955 continued into 1960, in interstate transportation. Segregation of buses and trains and interstate transportation facilities was against federal law, but local officials often ignored the law.

In many places, white and black passengers could not sit together on buses and trains. Waiting areas of bus and train stations had separate sections—one area for white passengers, another area for black passengers. A black passenger who boarded a bus in a northern state was forced to obey Jim Crow laws when the bus entered most southern states.

After the success of the sit-ins, students designed a new strategy to change segregated interstate travel. James Farmer, the director of the Congress of Racial Equality (CORE), was a veteran of the civil rights movement. Under Farmer's leadership, CORE had worked to integrate interstate transportation since 1947. In 1961, members of CORE

Like many public transportation centers, the Memphis, Tennessee, bus station had segregated waiting rooms for passengers. *(Library of Congress)*

Freedom Riders look at a map of their trip. From left to right: Edward Blankenheim, James Farmer, Genevieve Hughes, Rev. B. Elton Cox, and Henry Thomas, a student from St. Augustine, Florida. *(Martin Luther King, Jr., Library/*Washington Star *Collection)*

joined forces with the Student Nonviolent Coordinating Committee to begin the Freedom Rides. The Freedom Riders were groups of whites and blacks who rode buses through southern states to challenge segregation in interstate transportation. Twelve people volunteered to participate in the first Freedom Ride. Like the sit-in demonstrators, the Freedom Riders went through training in nonviolence. Their ages ranged from seventeen to sixty-one. Many, like

50

John Lewis and Ed Blankenheim, were veterans of the sit-ins. The first group to go on a Freedom Ride also included James Peck; Dr. Walter Bergman; Frances Bergman; Reverend B. Cox; Albert Bigelow; Hank Thomas, a college student; Charles Person; Genevieve Hughes; Jimmy McDonald; and Joe Perkins. The protestors planned to integrate waiting areas, lunch counters, and bathrooms in the bus stations as well as seating on buses. They agreed that if arrested, they would not pay bail—instead they would go to jail.

The 1961 Freedom Riders began their trip in Washington, D.C., and proceded south. The first group of Freedom Riders was followed by a second group on another bus. They planned to ride through Virginia, North Carolina, South Carolina, Georgia, Alabama, Mississippi, Louisiana, Arkansas, Florida, and Texas.

The first group traveled to stops in Virginia and North Carolina, where minor incidents of harassment occurred. A couple of the riders were arrested as they attempted to desegregate lunch counters at bus stations. But the real trouble began in Alabama.

In Birmingham, the Freedom Riders were attacked by angry white protesters. Violence erupted again on May 14, 1961, when a mob surrounded the bus a few miles outside of the small town of Anniston, Alabama. The mob began to attack the bus with baseball bats and clubs. Someone threw a bomb into a window, and as the Freedom Riders jumped off the burning bus they were beaten. Police officers merely stood by and watched. The mob also attacked the second

51

Diane Nash

I felt that it was critical that the Freedom Rides should continue, even after the violence in Montgomery and Anniston. To stop the rides would send the wrong message to civil rights activists and to the entire country—that violence could put an end to the civil rights movement. After those incidents it was not difficult to get other people to volunteer to participate in the rides. There were only three requirements to qualify: You had to be committed to nonviolence; you had to participate in workshops that taught you how to respond if you were attacked; and, finally, the unspoken requirement was that you had to be willing to sacrifice your life because—as Anniston and Montgomery proved—you could be hurt or killed. Often, as the Freedom Riders boarded their buses to begin their journey, they would hand me letters to give to their loved ones just in case something happened. As the elected coordinator of the Freedom Rides, I was responsible for talking to the Justice Department, concerned relatives, civil rights organizations, and the press. We got pressure from everyone to stop. No one quite understood why we wanted to complete the Rides.

bus when it arrived in Anniston. Protestors boarded the bus and began to hit the Freedom Riders. Dr. Walter Bergman was brutally beaten. Again, the police refused to protect the

We, on the other hand, couldn't understand why we had to wait for freedom.

Ending discrimination is not only a struggle to change laws. Internal liberation is just as important. What you think and feel about differences in races or religions is just as important as your actions.

I don't believe that voting is enough. Many people think that it is. The five minutes you spend in the voting booth is not nearly enough to exercise a person's responsibilities in a government or in a community. Reading, writing, and talking are not enough, either. All of it must be balanced with action. You will think differently as a result of having worked for social change. There is no way you can skip that—you must really work for social change. Youth should take very seriously who they are as people, and that has to be an ever-unfolding experience. Some children seem to be lost now. I think it is important to take truth very seriously. It's most important to be truthful with yourself about everything—not just to try to be good, you should do it because it gives you accurate information on which to base your life and your decisions.

Diane Nash resides in Chicago. She lectures about civil rights and feminism on college campuses across the country.

demonstrators. Fearing for the safety of the demonstrators, CORE ended the first Freedom Ride.

A few days later, a second round of Freedom Rides began. New demonstrators quickly replaced the injured. Eighteen-year-old Diane Nash, a member of SNCC and already a veteran of the sit-in demonstrations, served as a coordinator. She organized students to take the places of the original Freedom Riders. If they had any trouble while traveling they called her and she arranged for help.

When the bus arrived in Montgomery, Alabama, hundreds of white protestors surrounded it. As the Freedom Riders got off the bus, the angry mob assaulted and badly hurt many of them. Despite the violence, the Freedom Rides continued with new recruits, mostly college students, eager to join the struggle. President John F. Kennedy ordered the police to protect the students. As Freedom Riders were arrested and injured, other students quickly took their places.

The Freedom Rides continued all summer as Freedom Riders spread their cause to other types of transportation, including trains and planes. Many people of different ages, blacks as well as whites, journeyed on the Freedom Rides. A large number went to jail, where they were often attacked and beaten. Many were also forced to work twelve hours a day while in jail, and spend time in solitary confinement.

But people were still willing to make great personal sacrifices because they realized that the civil rights struggle had not been completely won. After the Freedom Rides, many students realized how much civil rights work remained to be done, especially in Mississippi and Alabama. The ranks of the civil rights movement increased as more people became involved. Students joined the struggle for
54 freedom in increasing numbers, and at even younger ages.

S E V E N

The Children's Crusade

"Nevertheless, the spirit of self-sacrifice and commitment
remains firm, and the state governments find themselves
dealing with students who have lost the fear of
jail and physical injury."

—Martin Luther King, Jr.

The children filed out of the Sixteenth Street Baptist
Church in Birmingham, Alabama, clapping and
singing, their voices filling the air:

> We shall overcome
> We shall overcome
> We shall overcome someday
> Deep in my heart
> I do believe
> We shall overcome someday

The church was surrounded by police officers. When
the children marched to the barricades that encircled the
church, the police moved in, swinging billy clubs. As the
police began to arrest them, some children knelt and
prayed, some laughed, and others clapped as they were
placed in the police paddy wagons.

Then a second group of children emerged from the

As the students filed out of the Sixteenth Street Baptist Church in Birmingham, Alabama, they were met by police officers who ordered them to stop their demonstration. (Birmingham News/*Birmingham Public Library, Birmingham, Alabama*)

church. They, too, began to sing. As they watched their friends being handcuffed and led away to jail, their voices became louder, their words clear to everyone:

> We'll walk hand in hand
> We'll walk hand in hand someday
> Deep in my heart
> I do believe
> We'll walk hand in hand someday

When children refused to end their Children's Crusade in Birmingham, Alabama, they were arrested, placed in police vans, and taken to jail. (Birmingham News/*Birmingham Public Library, Birmingham, Alabama*)

A third group of children filled out of the church, shouting "Freedom Now!" and other slogans. They waved signs and banners.

Some of the children marched beyond the barriers into Kelly Ingram Park, across the street from the church. With hundreds of children to arrest, the police called in school buses to replace the overflowing paddy wagons.

The Children's Crusade began in Birmingham on May 2,

1963. Many of the children who took part were very young; some were only six years old. More than five hundred children were arrested and jailed in one of the most important demonstrations in the history of the civil rights movement.

Birmingham is one of the largest cities in the South, a major industrial center where different types of steel products are manufactured. Until 1966, it was also one of the most segregated cities in the United States.

In the early 1960s the federal government ordered city officials to integrate public facilities. But instead of obeying the order, the city chose to close parks, playgrounds, and swimming pools rather than allow integration.

Every time community leaders gathered to discuss the racial problems of Birmingham, members of the Ku Klux Klan broke up the meetings and beat the community leaders. Many bombings occurred in black neighborhoods. Black people were often mistreated by police officers. Restaurants remained segregated, and WHITE ONLY and COLORED signs were displayed at water fountains.

Martin Luther King, Jr.; Fred Shuttlesworth, a local minister; and other leaders of the civil rights movement decided to begin demonstrations in Birmingham because of the city's reputation for violence and discrimination against black people.

At that time, some Birmingham police, like many police officers in several southern cities, were also members of hate groups, and would not obey federal orders to desegregate. The Birmingham police chief, Eugene "Bull" Connor, warned that anyone who participated in civil rights demonstrations would be jailed. City officials also issued a law declaring that any civil rights leaders who encouraged people to participate in sit-ins or demonstrations would be arrested.

James Bevel, a former member of the Student Nonviolent Coordinating Committee (SNCC), served as an advisor to Martin Luther King, Jr. Bevel, King, and Shuttlesworth planned special demonstrations to end Jim Crow laws in Birmingham. Although many black adults knew that the laws were unfair, they were afraid that if they marched and went to jail, they could lose their jobs.

On April 12, during the first Birmingham protests, Dr. King and other civil rights leaders were arrested. Dr. King was separated from the other prisoners and put in solitary confinement. While Dr. King was in jail, he wrote a long letter to other ministers explaining why the demonstrations were necessary. The letter from the Birmingham city jail was published in many newspapers, and people all around the United States read it:

My dear Fellow Clergymen,
    While confined here in the Birmingham city jail, I came across your recent statement calling our present activities "unwise and untimely." . . .
    I think I should give the reason for my being in Birmingham. . . .
    . . . I am in Birmingham because injustice is here. . . .
    . . . One day the South will recognize its real heroes. . . . They will be the young high school and college students, young minis-

59

ters of the gospel and a host of their elders . . . carrying our whole nation back to those great wells of democracy which were dug deep by the Founding Fathers in the formulation of the Constitution and the Declaration of Independence."

People involved in the movement became discouraged that the man they considered their leader was in jail. Many stopped demonstrating because they worried that the demonstrations would hurt Dr. King's chance for release. Dr. King remained in jail for nine days before he was freed pending a court appeal.

While Dr. King was in jail, James Bevel began planning the children's marches.

Bevel was an organizer with the Southern Christian Leadership Conference (SCLC). He was also involved in the sit-in movement in Nashville, Tennessee. He knew the importance of involving students in the civil rights struggle, so he proposed that children be allowed to participate in the protest marches. Other civil rights leaders disagreed, because they did not want the children to be hurt. Bevel invited children to workshops on civil rights. Children heard about these workshops in church, at school, or from their friends and parents. In the workshops the children learned about the civil rights demonstrations that were occurring all around the United States. A film they saw showed children from other cities participating in nonviolent sit-ins and marches. The children in the film did not fight back when the police and angry mobs attacked them. At the conclusion

60   of the workshops, most of the Birmingham children decided

Martin Luther King, Jr., spent nine days in the Birmingham city jail. *(Flip Schulke/Black Star)*

that they, too, wanted to become involved in demonstrations to end segregation. Now they just had to wait their turn to march and protest.

On May 3, 1963, the second day of the demonstrations, even more young children gathered to march. Most of them knew their friends had been jailed and that they themselves risked arrest. Some of the children were afraid, but they believed that they had to help end discrimination and segregation in Birmingham.

Again, freedom songs and slogans filled the air as more than a thousand children marched out of Sixteenth Street Baptist Church. Their anxious parents waited in the park. When they marched down the street, police cars and fire engines blocked their path. The police officers had snarling dogs. The firemen pointed fire hoses in their direction. Suddenly the singing stopped. For a few seconds there was silence, and then the children began to sing again.

"Let them have it!" Police Chief Bull Connor hollered.

Fire fighters turned their hoses on the young demonstrators. The tremendous force of the water pushed the children to the ground. Screams filled the air as police dogs attacked them, biting them and tearing at their clothes. Many of the frightened children tried to run away, but the police officers hit them with billy clubs. Parents tried to rescue their children as the injured fell to the ground. Some children were hurt badly; others were arrested.

62 Another demonstration was held on May 4.

Police in Birmingham used water hoses in an attempt to force the young demonstrators to turn around. (Birmingham News/*Birmingham Public Library, Birmingham, Alabama*)

After three days, more than two thousand demonstrators, most of them children, had been arrested and sent to the Birmingham jail. Many others were hospitalized. Civil rights leaders threatened to boycott Birmingham's stores if segregation continued in the city. But store owners did not want a boycott because they needed the business of black customers. The police chief's brutal actions were hurting the city's image and keeping people away.

Television, newspaper, and magazine reporters from all **63** over the world came to Birmingham. Across the nation, people read and listened to news reports and saw pictures of children being beaten by police officers and attacked by dogs. Many people were horrified.

Violence increased in the city; homes in black neighborhoods were bombed. Some adults and a few young people did not remain nonviolent—they threw rocks at police officers. The violence that erupted in Birmingham disturbed many civil rights activists. This was one of the few times that some demonstrators fought back, ignoring directions to remain nonviolent.

Finally, on May 10, a plan to desegregate was announced. City officials and store owners would desegregate stores and hire black people to work in the stores.

The campaign in Birmingham was successful because of the Children's Crusade. Local parks and playgrounds were desegregated, black employees were hired, and WHITE ONLY signs were removed from some lunch counters. The young people who joined the civil rights struggle in Birmingham served as witnesses to freedom, courageous examples for adults and children all over the world.

EIGHT

The March for Jobs and Freedom

"You have awakened on hundreds of campuses
throughout the land a new spirit of social inquiry to the
benefit of all Americans."

—Martin Luther King, Jr.
Congressional Record 105
(20 May 1959): 8696–97

For weeks everyone talked about the March on Washington for Jobs and Freedom. Eight-year-old Raymond Greene heard people discussing it in school and in church. Raymond was glad that the march was going to be in Washington, D.C., his hometown. It was a great city with many wonderful things to see.

The large statue of President Lincoln was among his favorites. From the Lincoln Memorial he could see the long, wide reflecting pool. Raymond liked to draw. Sometimes he sat on the steps leading to the Memorial to sketch the beautiful cherry blossoms that bloomed in springtime on the trees around the Mall. He closed his eyes and tried to imagine the Mall filled with people.

It would not be the first time a civil rights march had

Raymond Greene's neighborhood was a few miles from the place where the March on Washington was held. *(Raymond Greene)*

taken place in the nation's capital. In the 1940s, Asa Philip Randolph, founder of the Brotherhood of Sleeping Car Porters, an organization that protected the rights of black people who worked for the railroad companies, planned a mass march in Washington to protest discrimination against black workers in defense plants during World War II. To prevent the demonstration, President Franklin D. Roosevelt ordered an end to the discrimination, and guaranteed increased employment of blacks.

In the 1950s, A. Philip Randolph organized several youth marches in Washington, D.C., and New York City to support desegregation of public schools. The first march was held in October 1958. Ten thousand people, mostly students, marched in the nation's capital. The next year, in April 1959, Randolph sponsored a second Youth March for Integrated Schools, and twenty-six thousand people attended. Along with other civil rights leaders, Dr. Martin Luther King, Jr., spoke to a crowd of mostly black high school and college students. The students came to show support for the 1954 *Brown* v. *Board of Education* decision against racial segregation in the nation's public schools. The demonstrators had collected thousands of signatures in support of the immediate integration of public schools across the country. The students' determination and struggle motivated adults to join the civil rights movement.

In the early 1960s, the unemployment rate of black Americans was double that of white Americans. Randolph pro-

Raymond Greene

The reflection pool and the Lincoln Memorial was and still is one of my favorite places. I still remember the day of the march how I looked into the pool and saw all of the different faces of people and how their reflections made it appear like these people were looking up at me. Some people sat at the edge of the pool and soaked their feet in the cool water. Although many people traveled long distances and were tired, everyone was kind and patient and spoke to one another. Everybody took pride in the march and in the distance and length of their trips to Washington, D.C. Many carried signs that revealed where they were from: Hawaii, California, Maine, Georgia, and Mississippi.

posed holding a march for jobs and freedom. At every train stop, members of the Brotherhood of Sleeping Car Porters told people to come to the big march. Bayard Rustin helped Randolph plan the march. Rustin was an organizer who assisted Martin Luther King, Jr., in Montgomery and also was helpful in organizing the Freedom Rides. The goal of the March on Washington was the passage of the Civil Rights Act—a law that would guarantee equal rights for all citizens of the United States regardless of the color of their skin.

68 Using the Youth March for Integrated Schools as a model,

I also remember a lot of children there, some younger than me, sitting on the shoulders of their fathers. Babies were cradled in their mothers' arms. I had never seen that many people in my life.

I don't remember any of the speeches. I don't remember hearing King's speech—my mother read it to me later. I do remember people's reactions. I especially remember the clapping; it sounded like thunder. The amazing thing is that the people who weren't on the podium, who really didn't get to say a word, made the march a part of history. Just by being there each and every one was saying yes to jobs and yes to freedom.

Raymond Greene is the project coordinator of a program to help homeless children in Washington, D.C.

Randolph organized the March on Washington the same way. Most people learned of the march through their church or school. Randolph knew that student participation was important. If students were involved the march would almost certainly be a success.

August 28, 1963, was a day for dreams to come true. More than two hundred and fifty thousand people gathered in Washington to participate in one of the largest demonstrations in the history of the United States. Thousands of elementary, junior high, high school, and college students

More than ten years after the student boycott of R. R. Moton High School, residents of Prince Edward County attended the March on Washington. *(Martin Luther King, Jr., Library/Washington Star Collection)*

participated. Students from R.R. Moton High School in Farmville, Virginia, attended. White and black people, young and old, came from every state, riding in trains, buses, and cars, sometimes traveling for many hours to get to Washington, D.C.

Martin Luther King, Jr., joined civil rights leaders from across the country in front of the Lincoln Memorial. Hundreds of people stood alongside the long reflecting pool. Some people even placed their tired feet in the cool water of the pool. Others climbed trees so they could get a better view of the speakers. When Dr. King took the stage, the crowd listened intently as he delivered the words to his famous "I Have a Dream" speech:

> So let freedom ring from the prodigious hilltops of New Hampshire.
> Let freedom ring from the mighty mountains of New York.
> Let freedom ring from the heightening Alleghenies of Pennsylvania.
> Let freedom ring from the snowcapped Rockies of Colorado.
> Let freedom ring from the curvaceous slopes of California.
> But not only that.
> Let freedom ring from Stone Mountain of Georgia.
> Let freedom ring from Lookout Mountain of Tennessee.
> Let freedom ring from every hill and molehill of Mississippi, from every mountainside, let freedom ring.
> And when we allow freedom to ring, when we let it ring from every village and hamlet, from every state and city, we will be able to speed up that day when all of God's children—black men and white men, Jews and Gentiles, Catholics and Protestants—will be able to join hands and to sing in the words of the old Negro spiritual, "Free at last, free at last; thank God Almighty, we are free at last."

Despite the success of the March on Washington, where thousands of black and white people gathered in nonviolent protest, the violence continued. Just a few days after that march, on September 15, 1963, violence claimed the lives of four children.

It was Youth Day at the Sixteenth Street Baptist Church in Birmingham, Alabama. Four young black girls were a part of the special celebration. Denise McNair and Cynthia Wesley, both thirteen, and Addie Mae Collins and Carole Robertson, ages fourteen, were very excited about the day's events. They talked as they quickly changed into their white choir robes. They were members of the Sixteenth Street Baptist Church children's choir. Summer was almost over, and in a couple of weeks school would begin. Just as the four girls finished dressing a bomb exploded. The steps leading to the basement collapsed. The entire church filled with smoke and screams as people tried to escape.

But Denise, Addie, Cynthia, and Carole could not escape. They were trapped beneath the collapsed basement. The bombing of the Sixteenth Street Baptist Church and the murder of four innocent children enraged many people. Crowds of angry protesters filled the streets of Birmingham. To disperse the crowds, police officers fired guns over the demonstrators' heads. A young black boy was accidently shot and killed. Another young boy was killed as he rode his bike with a friend.

Congress responded to the hatred and discrimination by passing the Civil Rights Act in 1964. The Civil Rights Act is a group of laws that makes it illegal to discriminate against anyone because of their race, religion, or sex.

Although it was now against the law for any public place to discriminate, the passage of the Civil Rights Act did not end the violence. In Mississippi, the Ku Klux Klan and Citizens Council continued to use violence against black people. But this did not stop the spirit of brotherhood from

72   spreading to Mississippi and Alabama.

Black and white students from civil rights organizations such as the Congress of Racial Equality (CORE) and the Student Nonviolent Coordinating Committee (SNCC) went into Mississippi to educate residents about voting. They lived with black residents who sometimes did not have large houses or a lot of food, but who opened their homes to the students. Student workers from CORE and SNCC set up community centers and schools that were called Freedom Schools. Because of the Freedom Schools, local students became more active in civil rights; learning about the success of the sit-ins and the Freedom Rides inspired them to help the movement more.

The Freedom Schools were started so that the residents of Mississippi could come together to talk about the problems in their communities and in the state. The schools were held in small rooms during the hot summer months, but the rooms were always filled as people learned about voting, the next major battle in the civil rights movement.

N I N E

The Road to Freedom

"By coming here you have shown yourselves to be highly
alert, highly responsible young citizens. And very
soon the area of your responsibility will increase, for
you will begin to exercise your greatest privilege as an
American—the right to vote."

—Martin Luther King, Jr.
Congressional Record 105
(20 May 1959): 8696–97

Eight-year-old Sheyann Webb lived in the George
Washington Carver Homes directly behind Brown
Chapel African Methodist Episcopal Church, in
Selma, Alabama. Sheyann was a member and attended
church every Sunday. On January 11, 1965, Sheyann noticed
a large crowd of people gathering in front of the church. Immediately she knew something was wrong. She stared at the
crowd. Some of the people she recognized as her neighbors,
but some were strangers, white people whom Sheyann had
never seen before. As they began to enter the church,
Sheyann followed them, sliding into a seat in the back of the
church where no one would notice her. Sheyann knew she
might be late for school, but she wanted to know what was
going on.

The meeting was to discuss voting rights. Sheyann's parents couldn't vote because they were black. Less than two hundred of the fifteen thousand black people living in Selma were registered to vote. Although voting would allow black Americans to elect government representatives who would share and express their concerns, registering to vote was difficult for black people in Selma. Many times they were beaten, or the registrar, the person who allowed someone to sign up to vote, gave black people a literacy test while white people did not have to take any tests. Sometimes black applicants were forced to pay a poll tax, an enormous amount of money that most people could not afford.

Hosea Williams, an aide to Dr. King, announced a plan to hold a march to increase voter registration, even though black people were not allowed to gather together in groups. Two days of every month were designated Registration Days, but the black residents of Selma changed the name to Freedom Days. Demonstrations would be held on Freedom Days, led by Dr. Martin Luther King, Jr.

Sheyann arrived at school five hours late. Her teacher, Mrs. Bright, was very upset.

"Sheyann, do you know what time it is? Where have you been, young lady?" she asked.

Embarrassed, Sheyann bit her bottom lip before answering. "I was at the church."

"Young lady, do you know how much trouble you're in? That meeting is for adults to talk about voting rights. There

75

African-Americans lined up to register to vote after President Lyndon B. Johnson signed the Voting Rights Act. (Birmingham News/*Birmingham Public Library, Birmingham, Alabama*)

is going to be a lot of trouble; you better stay away from that church."

Sheyann bit her lip even harder, but she couldn't hold back the tears any longer.

That night she told her mother about what had happened. Her mother was very worried. Sheyann's fifteen-year-old sister, Vivian, had been arrested and placed in jail after participating in a civil rights demonstration the year before. Sheyann's mother didn't want another child—and especially such a young one—to go to jail. The next day Sheyann told her best friend, Rachel, about the meeting at Brown Chapel and the plan for future mass meetings about voting. Sheyann went to every meeting, and sometimes Rachel went with her. Often they were the only two children to attend.

Hosea Williams encouraged Sheyann to learn freedom songs so that she could sing at some of the rallies. On Sunday morning in church, Sheyann found herself standing in front of more than five hundred people. She was very nervous. Her palms were sweaty; her mouth was dry. The first demonstration was planned for Monday, the next day. She looked out into the audience and saw some of her classmates and teachers. Rachel was sitting in the front row. The words tumbled out of her mouth . . .

"Ain't gonna let nobody turn me around . . ."

As she continued singing, Rachel joined her, and the rest of the church started to sing the freedom song.

On January 18, Sheyann marched in her first demonstra-   **77**

Sheyann Webb

I was involved in the civil rights movement because if you were a part of a church, and that church was a part of the civil rights movement, then you really didn't have a choice. I missed a lot of school during the demonstrations in Selma, but I got a different type of education. I think everyone was concerned about that, but eventually everyone understood why I was so involved. I was very lucky because Dr. King often spoke at our church. He was an inspiration; he made you feel like you could help to bring about change. That first day I felt almost hypnotized because Hosea Williams was talking about what was right and what was wrong, and while I didn't understand everything, I understood that. I sat for five hours listening, and I just decided that I wanted to be a part of the movement. My mother was frightened for me. I was afraid, too, because we all knew what had happened to the four little girls in Birmingham. But my parents didn't talk about fear and danger. It was just

tion. The second march was held the following day. Dr. King led more than two hundred fifty people in a demonstration to the courthouse to register to vote. Sheyann was paired with Mrs. Margaret Moore, a neighbor. The demonstrators were attacked by police officers, who hit them with billy clubs. Mrs. Moore held Sheyann's hand tightly as the

something that you sensed; you could see the expressions on their faces. Now that I think about it, I know I had to be crazy to get involved because of the danger, but that is the innocence of a child.

I was in my ballet class when I heard the news that Dr. King had been shot. I remember everybody staring at me. No one said anything, and then a television announcer came on the air and said that King was dead. I ran to my mother and hugged her, but I couldn't cry. We went home and I went to my room and wrote a poem about my pal, Dr. King. The next morning when I woke up, I kept wishing that it was all a dream. I started to cry and I couldn't stop.

Now, looking back on it, I think that so many children were involved in the civil rights movement because of the way that time was. We were all just ordinary kids who wanted freedom.

Sheyann still resides in Selma, Alabama. She graduated from Tuskegee Institute. She remains active in community affairs and travels all over the country to talk about the civil rights movement and the importance of education.

little girl was pushed by people trying to run away. Many of the demonstrators were arrested. Sheyann felt lucky she was not put in jail.

Sheyann often skipped school to attend the rallies, and sometimes she joined the demonstrators after school. On February 1, 1965, Dr. King led a group of schoolteachers in another march. For some of the teachers, this was their first march. Dr. King and the teachers were arrested when they reached the courthouse. When some of Selma's black schoolchildren heard that Dr. King and many of their teachers had been jailed, they decided to march to protest their arrests. Most of the children were in junior high school. Sheyann was one of the youngest students to participate. Clapping and marching, the children showed their pride in their teachers and Dr. King. As they reached the courthouse, the police stopped them. At least three hundred children were jailed.

A few days later, the students, teachers, and Dr. King were released. Some of the white citizens of Selma held their own demonstration to support the civil rights marchers. They also believed that the voter-registration laws were unfair.

On February 18, 1965, a nighttime demonstration turned violent. A young black man, Jimmie Lee Jackson, was killed as he tried to protect his grandfather and mother from the police and an angry mob.

To protest Jimmie Lee Jackson's death, Dr. King announced a fifty-mile march from Selma, where Jimmie Lee Jackson was killed, to the state capitol in Montgomery. Sheyann had met Jimmie Lee Jackson at one of the mass meetings. She remembered his kind, gentle smile. Suddenly she felt sad, angry, and afraid. She didn't want to be shot or killed. Sheyann was so confused she didn't know what to

think.

On Sunday, March 7, the day of the big demonstration, Sheyann woke up with a headache. She couldn't keep Jimmie out of her mind, and she was still frightened.

"You don't have to march," her mother said as she combed Sheyann's hair.

"No, I'm going because I want to be free," Sheyann replied.

Her mother hugged her. "You know, I am very proud of you. You're growing up." Sheyann smiled. She was nine years old now, but she felt a lot older.

There wasn't any trouble until the civil rights demonstrators approached the Edmund Pettus Bridge, heading out of Selma. A large group of local police and state police officers moved toward the demonstrators. The officers rode their horses into the crowds and attacked the marchers with sticks and electric cattle prods. Sheyann joined the demonstrators as they kneeled and began to pray.

Shots rang out. The air filled with tear gas, and her eyes began to sting. As people ran, screaming, Sheyann ran too. Suddenly someone picked her up and carried her away from the police officers.

The day became known as "Bloody Sunday." People around the world watched on television as innocent protestors, including children, were beaten. Hundreds were injured and taken to hospitals.

That night at the voting rights rally, Sheyann listened as Dr. King promised that they would continue the struggle. Her eyes were still puffy and red from the tear gas and from crying, but she knew that if Dr. King and others continued to protest she would too.

Soon people from all over the United States came to Selma to join the voting rights protests.

On March 21, demonstrators began to march once again from Selma to Montgomery. More than four thousand people, black and white, young and old, began the march in Selma. Soon thousands of other marchers joined them. Five days later, the demonstrators reached Montgomery, and more than twenty-five thousand people marched up to the state capitol.

Less than six months later, President Lyndon Baines Johnson signed the Voting Rights Act into law. He said: "The vote is the most powerful instrument ever devised by man for breaking down injustice. . . ." The Voting Rights Act declared that everyone, regardless of race or religion, had the constitutional right to cast a vote in any public election or to determine any and all public resolutions.

The civil rights movement had won its most important battle. Black Americans were now guaranteed the right to elect candidates to any public office, to serve *all* of the people.

After Dr. King left Montgomery and moved to Atlanta, Georgia, he continued to participate in the major events of the civil rights movement. He and his wife, Coretta, had three more children: Martin Luther King, III, Dexter Scott, and Bernice Albertine.

82   King was deeply committed to his family, but he was also

The Selma-to-Montgomery marchers were met by mobs who wanted to stop the peaceful demonstration. (Birmingham News/*Birmingham Public Library, Birmingham, Alabama*)

committed to the civil rights struggle. He went to Birmingham; Selma; Albany, Georgia; Chicago; and many other cities to lead demonstrations. Sometimes he was attacked by angry mobs and sometimes he was thrown in jail, but he continued to preach nonviolence.

Some black leaders no longer believed that nonviolence could work. Sometimes, demonstrations ended in violence, and demonstrators were killed or hurt.

In February 1968, Dr. King visited Montgomery again. He

83

During a 1990 ceremony commemorating the 1965 Selma-to-Montgomery march, **Sheyann Webb** was carried off the Edmund Pettus Bridge in Selma by Spiver **Gordon, left; Hosea Williams, center; and Georgia Congressman John Lewis, right.** *(AP/Wide World Photos)*

spent time with Sheyann and her family. Sheyann was then twelve years old. She had changed a lot, just as the country had changed. She was glad to see Dr. King. He seemed tired, but he talked about plans for future civil rights demonstrations, such as the Poor People's Campaign, a plan to

84

help both needy white and black Americans. As he left her home, he picked Sheyann up and hugged her. It was the last time Sheyann would see him.

In April 1968, Dr. King went to Memphis, Tennessee. Black sanitation workers had invited him there to lead a demonstration for better wages. On April 4, 1968, as he stood on the balcony of his room at the Lorraine Motel in Memphis, he was assassinated by James Earl Ray. January 15 has been declared Martin Luther King, Jr., Day, a national holiday, in honor of the many contributions that he made to the civil rights movement.

AFTERWORD

The profiles in this book illustrate personal struggles in a movement for freedom. All the brave young students involved in the civil rights movement felt a sense of responsibility not only to themselves and their families, but also to their communities and to the nation. They were eager to contribute their time and energy, and sometimes their lives, for what they believed was right. At the center of the civil rights movement lay love and a deep belief in nonviolence. Through the students' stories, we have learned that a battle rooted in hatred cannot succeed.

The struggle to end discrimination, inequality, and injustice continues. You are a part of the struggles in our country and in the world. As you can see from this book, you don't have to wait until you're an adult to accept the challenge to end discrimination and injustice. Find ways to work together. Although we may be of different colors, cultures, races, and religions, we have a common goal—freedom. We must not allow differences to keep us apart. Instead, we must choose to understand and respect one another.

You have inherited the dream!

SOURCES

BOOKS

Bates, Daisy. *The Long Shadow of Little Rock.* New York: David Mc-
Kay Co., 1962.

Branch, Taylor. *Parting the Waters: America in the King Years,
1954–63.* New York: Simon and Schuster, 1988.

Garrow, David J. *Bearing the Cross: Martin Luther King, Jr., and the
Southern Christian Leadership Conference.* New York: Vintage
Books, 1986.

——*Protest at Selma: Martin Luther King, Jr., and the Voting Rights
Act of 1965.* New Haven, Conn.: Yale University Press, 1978.

Huckaby, Elizabeth. *Crisis at Central High: Little Rock, 1957–58.*
Baton Rouge, La.: Louisiana State University Press, 1980.

King, Jr., Martin Luther. *Strive Toward Freedom: The Montgomery
Story.* New York: Harper & Row, 1958.

Morris, Aldon D., *The Origins of the Civil Rights Movement.* New
York: Free Press, 1984.

Robinson, Jo Ann Gibson. *The Montgomery Bus Boycott and the
Women Who Started It.* Knoxville, Tenn.: University of Tennessee
Press, 1987.

Smith, Robert Collins. *They Closed Their Schools: Prince Edward
County, Virginia, 1951–1964.* Chapel Hill, N.C.: University of
North Carolina Press, 1965.

Webb, Sheyann, and Nelson, Rachel West. *Selma, Lord, Selma.* University, Ala.: University of Alabama Press, 1980.

SOURCES

Williams, Juan. *Eyes on the Prize: America's Civil Rights Years, 1954–1965*. New York: Viking Press, 1987.

Manuscript Collections

Civil Rights Documentation Project. Moorland-Spingarn Research Center, Howard University, Washington, D.C.

Papers of A. Philip Randolph, Library of Congress.

Papers of the Congress of Racial Equality (CORE), Library of Congress.

Papers of the National Association for the Advancement of Colored People (NAACP), Library of Congress.

FURTHER READING
FOR CHILDREN

Adler, David A., and Casilla, Robert. *Martin Luther King, Jr.: Free at Last*. New York: Holiday House, 1986.

De Kay, James T. *Meet Martin Luther King, Jr.* New York: Random House, 1989.

Greenfield, Eloise. *Rosa Parks*. New York: Crowell, 1973.

Haskins, James. *The Life and Death of Martin Luther King, Jr.* New York: Lothrop, Lee & Shepard, 1977.

Jackson, Florence. *Blacks in America, 1954–1979*. New York: Franklin Watts, 1980.

Kosof, Anna. *Jesse Jackson*. New York: Franklin Watts, 1987.

Levine, Ellen. *Freedom's Children*. New York: Putnam, 1992.

McKissack, Patricia, and McKissack, Fredrick. *The Civil Rights Movement in America from 1865 to the Present*. Chicago, Ill.: Children's Press, 1991.

Millender, Dharathula H. *Martin Luther King, Jr.: Young Man with a Dream*. New York: Macmillan, 1986.

Parks, Rosa, with James Haskins. *Rosa Parks: My Story*. New York: Dial Books for Young Readers, 1992.

Patterson, Lillie. *Martin Luther King, Jr., and the Freedom Movement*. New York: Facts on File, 1989.

Stein, R. Conrad. *The Story of the Montgomery Bus Boycott*. Chicago, Ill.: Children's Press, 1986.

Webb, Sheyann, and Nelson, Rachel West. *Selma, Lord, Selma*. University, Ala.: University of Alabama Press, 1980.

INDEX

Page numbers in *italics* refer to illustrations.

ABOUT THE AUTHOR

Author BELINDA ROCHELLE says: "Most of the books about the civil rights movement focus on the contributions of one person, yet the movement was successful because of many people. I wanted to write this book for children because it shows how children themselves can affect history."

Belinda Rochelle's poetry and articles have appeared in many magazines. She has served as a lobbyist and community organizer, providing information on public health policy to more than eight hundred community-based organizations in the United States and Africa. This is her first book.

Ms. Rochelle lives in Washington, D.C., with her daughter, Shevon.